Longhaired Cats

Grace Pond

Longhaired Cats

B. T. Batsford Ltd London

Photography by Paddy Cutts/Animals Unlimited

Frontispiece Blue and
Cream kittens: there
may well be some
future prizewinners
here; breeder Mrs
Pullen

ISBN 0 7134 4101 1

Typeset by Typewise Limited,
Wembley, Middlesex
and printed in Hong Kong
for the publishers
B. T. Batsford Ltd
4 Fitzhardinge Street
London W1H 0AH

Contents

1 The History of the Longhaired Cats

As far as can be ascertained, the first domesticated cats, for which Egypt is generally given the credit, had short fur, although there is still much mystery about their beginnings. There is just as much mystery about the origin of the cats with long coats. The Comte Georges de Buffon (1707-88), a French naturalist, wrote a book which was translated, abridged and published in England in 1792 as *Natural History*. In his book he included some pages on cats with long fur. He spoke of long-coated cats in Spain and also those in Chorafan and Syria, and went on to say that 'when wild cats are tamed their coats become longer, finer and most copious, with colour changes'. He believed that, by taking cats with the most white in their coats and with the longish fur, it was possible to produce the Angora to order. This is now known to be the first step in the selective breeding of longhairs. He wrote too of cats in China with long fur and pendant ears, which were great favourites with the Chinese ladies. His reference to the Angoras is one of the earliest; exactly when these cats and others with long fur, such as the Persians, first evolved is still a matter of surmise.

In all probability a kitten with a fluffy coat was born in a shorthaired litter; that is, it was a mutation, and because of its unusual appearance it was kept. Natural matings with a litter brother or sister or with the father could result in further such kittens. The strange thing is that this seems to have happened at about the same time in various parts of the world such as confined mountainous areas in Turkey, Persia (now Iran), China, India, Afghanistan and the Soviet Union. It is possible that there may have been such cats for centuries, but because of the inaccessibility of these areas, the few travellers reaching them, and the lesser interest in cats in comparison with the unusual larger wild animals, no mention was made of them until the sixteenth century. There are many stories and legends about the Siamese and similar cats being found in temples or in the royal courts, but of the longhairs only the Birmans were associated with a similar history.

Early travellers, pilgrims and seafarers must have been instrumental in bringing the first long-coated cats into Europe from the East. Pietro de la Velle is said to have introduced cats with long fur into Italy in the middle of the sixteenth century, and at the end of that century Nicholas Claude Fabri de Peirese, the naturalist, was responsible for bringing the Angora cats into France, where de Buffon must have seen them. Later these cats came into Britain, and were known as French cats, which seemed logical at the time!

In 1868 Charles Ross, an early writer on cats, gave details of the various longhaired breeds in Britain; this was before the first official show in 1872. He wrote that 'Angoras have silvery hair of a fine silken texture, but some are yellowish and others olive, approaching the colour of the lion'. The Persian cat, he wrote, had 'hair long and very silky, perhaps more so than the Cat of Angora, differently coloured being of a fine

Gr Ch Deebank Blackjack, a Black with an outstanding broad head. Owner Miss Jacqui Stevens; breeder Miss M.F. Bull.

7

Grand Champion Blue-eyed White — Chirunga Polarice, with his little pewter kitten. Owner and breeder Mrs Kayes

uniform grey on the upper part with the texture of the fur as soft as silk and the lustre glossy.' He said that the Chinese cat had beautifully glossed fur, variegated with black and yellow, and usually with pendulous ears, and referred to the Spanish cat or Tortoiseshell with fur of moderate length, with colours of pure black, white and reddish orange. Dr Gordon Stables, an author and early cat fancier, referred to the longhairs in his own book *The Domestic Cat* published in 1876, but called them the Asiatic cats. He wrote that they could be found in the same colours and variations in colour and markings as those of the shorthaired European cats, that is in blue, white, black and tabbies, all with 'long pelages and good brushes' (coats and tails).

The most famous cat expert of that time, and the man to whom the Cat Fancy all over the world owes its very being, was Harrison Weir, an artist, an author, and a Fellow of the Royal Horticultural Society. Not only was he responsible for the first official cat show ever held, but he drew up the Points of Excellence, now known as the standards, by which cats could be judged; he was also one of the first cat judges. In his book published in 1889, he gave details of the Angora, the Persian and the Russian; the latter, he said, had 'the woolliest coat of them all' and were 'mostly dark tabby'. In his Points he distinguished between the fur, 'being fine, silky and very soft in the Persian, slightly woolly texture in the Angora and still more so in the Russian.' Referring to the tails he said that those of the Persians had hair long and silky throughout, but somewhat longer at the base; the Angora was like the brush of a fox, but longer in the hair; and the Russian equally long in hair but more full at the end, 'tail shorter rather blunt, like a tassel'. From a mixture of these early longhairs, expert and planned breeding has produced in 100 years over 40 colour variations and coat patterns in the cats with long coats.

Such was the great public interest in the first cat show which was held at the Crystal Palace in 1871 that other shows followed rapidly, not only in Britain, but also in the United States of America, and eventually throughout the world. The breeding and showing of pedigree cats both long- and short-coated became fashionable, and Harrison Weir was rather dismayed when he realized that gradually his favourites, the English Shorthairs, now British Shorthairs, were losing their popularity to the cats from the East, the Longhairs.

In the early days of the Cat Fancy little was known about breeding for particular colours and as the cats from Persia had longer fur and broader heads with smaller ears, and the kittens in particular had 'chocolate box' appeal, they began to be preferred to the Angoras, with their smaller heads, larger ears and longer noses. There must have been cross-matings, as eventually the 'Angora' vanished and all the cats with long fur were known as 'Persians'. In fact one cat judge, the breeder and author Miss Frances Simpson, in her book *The Book of the Cat* (1902) wrote that 'the differences between Angoras and Persians are of so fine a nature that I must be pardoned if I ignore the class of cat commonly called Angora, which seems gradually to have disappeared from our midst.'

At the beginning of the century the colours recognized in Britain were:

15 Black
16 White
17 Blue
18 Orange (later to be called Red)
19 Cream (also referred to as Fawn)
20 Sable
21 Smoke
22 Tabby
23 Spotted
24 Chinchilla
25 Tortoiseshell
26 Bicolour
27 Tricolour

Whites were the most popular variety, but Blacks were comparatively few in number. The first Blues were shown in the 'Any Other Variety' classes as many had white patches and tabby markings. The cats known as Orange in most cases were really what are now known as Red Selfs or Red Tabbies. The Creams or Fawns were looked on as 'sports' or as pale Oranges to begin with, but when a little more was understood about breeding, they came into their own, were much improved in colour, and also were used to produce the Blue-Creams. There is hardly a reference anywhere to the Sables (Self Browns), which must have originated from lightly marked Brown Tabbies. They do not appear in the Stud Book and Register for 1900 - 1905 and seem to have vanished. Years later when the late Mr Brian Stirling Webb began selective breeding to produce the Colourpoints he realized that both Self Chocolates and Self Lilacs could be bred in the same programme. This has happened but it has taken some years to get the varieties recognized with full Championship status, and they are comparatively few in number.

Cross-matings between Blacks and Silvers (Chinchillas and Silver Tabbies) are said to have produced the original Smokes, which were far more numerous at the turn of the century then they are today. Harrison Weir gave the original Tabbies as Brown, Silver, Light Grey and White, with the colours as 'rich, reddish brown, bright deep rich even dark blue, the Silver lighter and equally even tint, light grey with pure white ground'. The Oranges or Reds were not mentioned in the Tabbies. Some were obviously difficult to produce, as in a very short time, the only colours recognized in the Tabbies were Brown, Silver and Red, all without White. Spotties with long coats, although now flourishing in the British Shorthairs in various colourings, are no longer seen. The Chinchillas are thought to have originated from lightly marked Silver Tabbies and Blues, but they were certainly of a different colouring from the magnificent specimens seen at the shows today. Miss Simpson wrote of these early Chinchillas as having 'the fur at the roots a peculiar light silver, not white...and this shades to a slightly darker tone — a sort of bluish lavender — at the tips of the coats'.

The Tortoiseshells, a female-only variety, had a standard similar to that of today, i.e. requiring the three colours black, orange and yellow, well broken and as bright as possible. Those cats seen at the early shows were entered in the 'Any Other Variety' classes and according to a female judge were not outstanding, although she complained that they were invariably given 'some mark of distinction' when they were judged by 'the professional men judges', as Tortoiseshells were the men's favourite breed. I might add that men seem still to like Torties today. Very few Bicolour or Pied cats appear to have been shown. They were probably in the 'Any Other Variety' classes and are therefore difficult to trace. For years they were not recognized, but comparatively recently fanciers realized that Bicolours would be very useful in breeding for Tortoiseshell-and-Whites, another female-only variety. One well-known breeder concentrated on producing them, and they now appear in a number of colours, and have full Championship status. The early Tortoiseshell-and-Whites were few and far between, as producing them was very much a matter of chance, and one judge said those she had seen should be called White-and-Tortie, as they had more white than anything.

These were the varieties seen at the early shows, and they were considered most exotic in their day. As the years have gone by the type has improved, and shorter, flatter noses have become fashionable. Some of today's cats, in fact, have noses that are too short, but this can be rectified by careful breeding.

Opposite Ryshworth Rumtumtugger, a male Red Self Longhair with a coat of a very striking colour. Owner and breeder Mrs Pam Sadler.

11

Red Tabby Longhair. Shown is Ch Ithilien Coriander, owned and bred by Mr and Mrs D. Spears.

In just 100 years since the beginning of the Britain's Cat Fancy, by accidental cross-matings and later by selective and planned breeding it has been possible to produce 40 longhair pedigree colourings and variations. The early varieties have in most cases been improved in type and colourings. Man-made varieties, such as the Colourpoints, have been bred, and the Turkish and the Birmans have been introduced by importation. Chocolates, the Lilacs, the Cameos and now the Pewters are all appearing on the show bench. Much improved knowledge of genetics, particularly in the last decade or two, has enabled breeders to produce specific colourings beyond the dreams of the early fanciers.

Typically patched
Tortoiseshell, Hopecott
Nicola: this is one of
the female-only
varieties. Owner and
breeder Mr and Mrs C.
Green.

2 Shows, Show Activity and the Cat Fancy

In 1871, in the reign of Queen Victoria (who later owned two Blue Persians), the first official cat show to be held anywhere in the world took place at the Crystal Palace in London. The show was the brainchild of Mr Harrison Weir, who felt that such an event would bring to the public the realization of how beautiful cats could be. He could never have visualized what he was starting, that in little more than 100 years cat shows would be held in most countries throughout the world, that cats and kittens would be exported from one country to another sometimes for sums involving quite a few hundred pounds or dollars and that there would be innumerable organizations providing cat foods, cat accessories and cat medication of various kinds.

When the doors opened on that July morning there were hundreds waiting to see the 170 cats and kittens that were being exhibited for the first time ever. These included Angoras, Persians, two Siamese and even a Wild Cat from Scotland, which had lost part of a front paw, and yet was still so fierce that a dozen men failed to get the poor creature out of its basket. The show was reported in full by newspapers, with the *Illustrated London News* including a number of drawn illustrations of many of the cats. There were complaints on the day that there were so many of the public there that for some it proved impossible to see the cats.

Mr Harrison Weir, his brother Jenner, and the Rev. Cumming Macdona judged the exhibits, and 54 prizes, with the grand total value of £57 15s, were awarded. The cats shown included Crimean cats, Prussian cats and Algerian cats as well as Persians. I presume that they came from these various countries, hence the names.

Such was the popularity of the first show, and the public demand, that another show was quickly organized in December. In the next few years there followed a spate of cat shows in such towns as Edinburgh, Crawley, Brighton, Manchester, and Birmingham as well as London. Soon shows were being held in the United States and other parts of the world. Quarantine regulations did not exist and it was possible to send cats and kittens from one country to another to be shown. In these early days there were no pedigree cats as such, for no records were kept of ancestry, and it was soon realized that to put everything on a proper basis it would be necessary to have some kind of register with details of breeding and parentage, and the different varieties.

In 1887 the National Cat Club came into being, with Mr Harrison Weir as the president and many august personages and members of society on the committee. The club started a register and was the world's first governing body, with cats and kittens being accepted at the shows only if they were registered, for which the charge was one shilling. The shows were held under the sponsorship of the

A cat may always be washing, but daily grooming is still necessary for the removal of loose hairs. This cat is being prepared for show.

National Cat Club and the charge for each class entered was 5 shillings, a lot of money in those days. Similar rulings applied then as today: cats would be disqualified if not registered, or if they had not been in the possession of the exhibitor for at least 14 days prior to the show, if the wrong pedigree was given or if the age of the cat or kitten was incorrectly given. Free use of powder on the coat would also mean disqualification as could 'dyeing the chins of tabby cats and the white spots on self colour cats', which would also certainly be the case today. Then, as now, the exhibits on arrival at the shows were examined by a qualified veterinary surgeon.

The first large American cat show was held in Madison Square Gardens, New York, in 1895. Organized by an Englishman, Mr J. Hyde, it followed similar lines to the Crystal Palace shows in Britain and was an immediate success. The Chicago Cat Club was founded in 1899 but was short-lived, being ousted by the Beresford Cat Club founded by Mrs Clinton Locke. It was named after the English breeder, Lady Marcus Beresford, who was interested in many varieties and frequently exported outstanding cats to the United States.

Until 1910 the National Cat Club was Britain's sole registering body and ran the Cat Fancy, but in 1898 a rival organization, called the Cat Club, was founded and held several shows. There followed a period of unrest and dissatisfaction, but eventually the Cat Club seems to have vanished, and differences were sorted out. In 1910 the National Cat Club handed over all its rights and governing powers to a council which was composed of delegates chosen from the various cat clubs which had come into being as the number of shows increased throughout the country. This was the Governing Council of the Cat Fancy, which is still the sole British governing and registering body today. The National Cat Club was granted the right to have four delegates in perpetuity on the Council.

The role of the GCCF is described in more detail later in this chapter.

At first cat breeding and exhibiting seemed to be purely the prerogative of the wealthy and of 'High Society', with fanciers such as the Lady Decies, who showed many longhaired cats including Ch Fulmer Zaida, winner of over 150 prizes, and the Lady Marcus Beresford, who was said to have about 150 cats, and travelled around the country to the various shows with a retinue of servants to look after them. The Hon. Mrs McLaren Morrison was well known for her Black cat 'Satan' and often exhibited 14 Blacks at one show. The patron of the National Cat Club was HRH Princess Victoria of Schleswig Holstein. As Queen Victoria herself visited shows with the Prince of Wales, later Edward VII, pedigree cats became 'status symbols', especially as the Princess of Wales, afterwards Queen Alexandra, was also a cat-lover. Later classes were put on for the 'Working Classes' at reduced fees and for pet cats only (it was felt that they would not be able to afford pedigree cats).

In those days there were no vaccinations or injections available to protect the cats and kittens from the killer diseases which were then prevalent. Frequently, after a show, fanciers would lose all their stock, never thinking to isolate the exhibit they were bringing home from the show. Often too, they would go and buy another kitten straightaway only to have this one die from the infection in a very short time. Death could come so swiftly that the owners were quite sure that their cats had been poisoned at the show. In the early days the judges never wore overalls to protect their clothing, as all British judges do today. Skirts were long, sweeping the ground, and hygiene was of a very low standard. World War I saw fewer shows and very little breeding, but by 1920 the Cat Fancy was beginning to pick up again, and more shows were held. The National Cat Club continued to hold its shows at the

Crystal Palace until 1936 when the building burned down the day before the show was due to be held. However, the show did go on in another hall after the show manager sent telegrams to everyone concerned, and it was its usual success.

Over the years more varieties were recognized and the Fancy flourished, many more fanciers taking up breeding and more clubs being formed. Unfortunately World War II nearly rang its death knell, hundreds of cats being put down by the often-reluctant vets and famous studs being neutered. Ever resilient, a few breeders managed to struggle on and they formed the nucleus of the now enormous Cat Fancy in Britain today. Shortly after the war ended the Notts and Derby Cat Club put on a cat show, but unfortunately many of the exhibits subsequently died from infection. The tragedy alerted fanciers again to the dangers of showing and shows were re-established very slowly. Fortunately in a year or two vaccines were being produced which did, and still do, keep some killer diseases to a minimum, and modern hygiene has also helped. Today it is not possible to exhibit at any show sponsored by the Governing Council of the Cat Fancy without a current certificate for protection against feline infectious enteritis for each cat and kitten shown. However, it is still wise to isolate an exhibit brought home from a show for some days rather than allowing it to mix straightaway with other cats, as there are still other illnesses, even a common cold, which can follow a show and can be given to other cats unless specific precautions are taken.

Should a cat prove difficult to handle at the show, it is unwise to keep showing. If a cat bites or seriously scratches a judge or steward a report has to be sent in by the show manager, and after three offences the cat will be banned from shows.

Whatever the show status the procedure is much the same for the would-be exhibitor.

Members of the club organizing the show are usually sent schedules, but non-members should send a stamped self-addressed envelope to the show manager at least two or three months before the date of the show. Any cat or kitten that is shown must have been registered with the GCCF and when it is purchased from the breeder, a transfer form must be completed and sent in with the appropriate fees to the registrar, at least three weeks before the cat is exhibited. With the schedule there will be an entry form which should be completed with details exactly as given on the kitten's registration form, and for the first show until it is known how the animal behaves when handled, it is better to enter only the Open breed class and about three others. In fact this is usually the minimum entry allowed. For a member of the club organizing the show, the fees are usually lower. An entry fee is payable for each class in addition to a benching fee covering the hire of the pen which will be used by the cat. Neuters may also be entered in a show and can ultimately win high honours. The exhibitor should try to choose classes with different judges, to get a number of opinions as to the animal's potentialities.

When sending in the entry form with the correct money, it is as well to enclose a self-addressed stamped card for the show manager to send back indicating that the entry has been accepted. If requested, a self-addressed envelope should also be included. This is for the tally and the vetting-in card which are sent a week or two before the actual show date, although a few shows give these out on the morning of the show. It is not essential to belong to the club running the show to enter.

The cat must be taken to the show in a basket or a box, and must never be carried in the arms. The numbered tally should be around the cat's neck on a narrow white ribbon or tape. Before being allowed into the hall, a veterinary surgeon will carry out a thorough examination.

Black Smoke — Ch Shirar Montgomery, showing glimpses of the contrasting undercoat. Owner and breeder Mr and Mrs G. Martin.

If, by any chance, the cat is running a high temperature, or has dirty ears or any signs of fleas in the fur, it will not be allowed to enter the hall, and all fees will be forfeit. Once past the vet and in the show hall, there will be rows of numbered pens, one of which will have the same number as the tally. It is as well to wipe the bars of the pen with cotton wool damped with a non-toxic disinfectant before putting the cat in. A warm white blanket, never a cellular one, should be put in the pen. If the weather is very cold a hot water bottle may be put under the blanket, well concealed. A plain white litter tray should be in the pen for sanitary purposes, and a small white container for drinking water. Nothing else is allowed. Food may be given about lunchtime, but anything that could be called an identifying object must not be there whilst judging is going on. When the word is given that the hall is to be cleared ready for the judges, the cat may be given a final brushing, but never powdered as this may mean disqualification. It should be checked that the correct tally is around the cat's neck and that the number is the same as on the pen, and then the owner should leave.

At the majority of the shows the halls are cleared and owners and public are not re-admitted until about mid-day. In some halls if there is a gallery, spectators are allowed to watch from there. At the National Cat Club show the exhibitors and the general public are allowed in all day, but the owner should never be near the cat's pen whilst he is being judged, and should certainly never speak to a judge until the judging is finished at the end of the day.

The judge's slips are placed on an award board in the hall, announcing the prizes. Prize cards and rosettes are placed on the pens, usually after lunch, and any prize monies awarded should be collected on the day, as it is not sent out afterwards.

Generally shows close about 5.30 p.m. On returning home, the cat should be given special attention, with the corners of the eyes, the mouth and ears, coat and paws being wiped with a very diluted and mild non-toxic disinfectant. Some fanciers advocate giving a little brandy or whisky in warm milk to the cat. A favoured food should be given and the cats kept away from other cats for a few days. Having been shut up in a pen all day probably the animal will rush around, glad to be out, but will soon settle down, and certainly will not be feeling quite as exhausted as the owner.

The Governing Council of the Cat Fancy is the sole registering body in Britain. The officers, the chairman, vice-chairman and treasurer are elected annually from the delegates. The entire Council meets four times a year, but there are a number of committees, meeting from time to time, such as the executive, the finance, the disciplinary, the genetics, standing orders and cat care, all of which are appointed to deal with the varying interests and aspects of the Cat Fancy. The executive meets practically every month to deal with the day-to-day running of the Council and Cat Fancy in general, and bring forward relevant items for the consideration and approval of the Council. The Council employs a paid secretary but all the officers and delegates are honorary. Four registrars are employed, one for Longhairs, one for Siamese, one for Shorthairs and one for Burmese.

The Council grants show licences, classifies cat breeds and varieties, approves the appointment of judges, and keeps registers of pedigree cats, issuing registration certificates and also registering the transfer of a cat from one owner to another, which must be done three weeks at least before a show if the new owner wishes to exhibit the cat. The Council approves prefixes, which are the cattery names registered in breeders' names. A prefix may only be used for kittens bred by a specific breeder, and once a kitten has been registered

The bustle of a modern cat show, the National Cat Club Show in 1982.

with a particular name this cannot be changed in any way, even if the kitten is going to a new owner.

A full cat, one that is not neutered, winning the Open or Breed Class at a show may be awarded a challenge certificate granted by the Council if the judges consider it is up to standard. A cat that is spayed or castrated, i.e. a neuter, may be awarded a premier certificate under the same conditions. If a cat wins three such certificates at three different shows under three different judges (if approved by the Council), it may become a Champion or if a neuter a Premier. A Champion cat may eventually become a Grand Champion or a neuter a Grand Premier by entering the Champion of Champions Class or the Premier of Premiers class. Three such wins under the same conditions as are given for challenge and

premier certificates may earn the cat the title of Grand Champion or Grand Premier. In the Champion of Champions class and the Premier of Premiers class there are no second or third prizes given — only a first and a reserve.

The Council approves and publishes Standards of Points, giving full details of the characteristics required for each recognized variety and the apportioning of the 100 points allocated for these.

From time to time, a Stud Book is published which gives the breeding and achievements of all the prize-winning cats at the shows, which is very useful for tracing pedigrees, and for choosing a cat to use as a stud. A booklet is also published giving details of the Council's constitution. After each show a marked catalogue is sent in by the show manager for checking. This is to make sure that all the details given by the exhibitors for their cats and kittens on the entry forms are correct. Should these differ from the animals' registration forms in any way it is possible that disqualification will follow. In these cases any rosettes, prize cards and monies won will have to be returned to the show manager. If an exhibitor fails to do this disciplinary action may be taken by the Council. Therefore it is very important for all exhibitors to double-check the details on the show entry form before posting.

The Council endeavours to improve cat breeding, to protect the welfare of cats and the interests of pedigree cat owners generally. It is never involved in the buying and selling of cats and kittens, nor in any financial arrangements made. All dates for shows have to be submitted to the Council, with details of the show manager and the venue, for approval and for the granting of a licence. The shows have to be conducted according to the rules set out by the Council.

All judges have to send in detailed reports of the exhibits to which they have awarded prizes for publication in *Cats*, the official organ of the GCCF.

In the earliest years of this century, the American Cat Association came into being as the first American registering body, very much in the same manner as did the National Cat Club in Britain. Over the years other associations, clubs and federations have been formed, with a number registering cats and sponsoring shows for their own associated clubs and societies.

These include the Cat Fanciers' Association, founded in 1906. Invariably known as the CFA, it is by far the largest registering body, having more than 400 member clubs and being responsible for more than half the vast number of shows held in the United States of America.

The great distances involved in the United States soon made it impracticable to have only one body registering and sponsoring shows

and others evolved: 1919 saw the formation of the Cat Fanciers' Federation (CFF); the United Cat Fanciers (UCF) was founded in 1946; the American Cat Fanciers' Association (ACFA) in 1955; the National Cat Fanciers' Association (NCFA) in 1960; the Crown Cat Fanciers' Federation (CCFF) in 1965; and the Independent Cat Federation (ICF) in 1969. The Canadian Cat Association (1961) is exclusively Canadian but several of the other associations hold shows in both the United States and Canada, while the CFA is also associated with certain shows in Japan. There are also a number of clubs not connected with any associations.

Several of the federations have banded together, being collectively known as the International Cat Associations. They accept cats registered with any association at their shows, which helps the exhibitors considerably; otherwise their cats must be registered with the specific organization running the show they wish to enter.

Fortunately the standards accepted are very much the same throughout North America, as is the system of running the shows, which differs considerably from that in Britain.

There are usually four separate shows going on at the same time, with four judges presiding. The judges do not go to the pens but sit at a table in judging rings, with chairs inside for the exhibitors watching the judging.

The cats are vetted-in and taken to the cages by the owners, who bring curtains to hang inside in colours complementary to the cats and put a thick coloured blanket or cushion in the bottom for the cat to sit on. Litter trays, food and water are usually provided by the management.

The classes that can be entered are few. The important ones are: the novice class for cats who have never won as an adult; the open class for those who already have a recorded win; the Champion for cats that hold four winners' ribbons; and Grand Champions — the winner of the last class is decided on a points' basis and

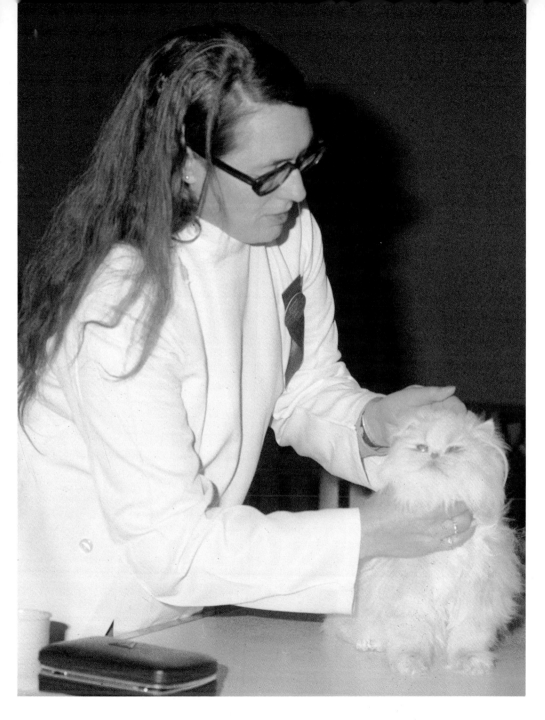

Vetting-in is the preliminary inspection of competitors, essential for the welfare of all cats at the show to avoid the spread of infection.

on the number of other Champions beaten. The classes are divided into 'colour' or variety classes and into male and female. Some associations have awards for the best cat in show, second best cat, best opposite-sex cat, best or opposite-sex Champion and Grand Champion. The CFA has a more simple arrangement now and chooses the five best cats.

When judging starts, the owner is called and takes the cat to the judge's table. The judge examines the cat thoroughly and the cat is then put in one of the ten empty pens behind her, while she marks up her judging sheet. She puts ribbons on the cages of the winners, blue, unlike in Britain, being the first-prize colour, with red for second.

Once a cat has been beaten it is returned to its own cage but the winners are judged against each other until eventually the best cat is found. Since in all probability four shows are going on at the same time in different rings, a cat may have been entered in the others and will be judged by a different judge, the system being exactly the same. It is therefore possible eventually for the same cat to be best in all the rings; on the other hand there may be four best cats chosen.

A kitten must be four months old to be shown in a kitten class and at eight months is considered to be old enough to enter the adult class.

The judges are paid according to the number of exhibits judged and receive travelling and hotel expenses. In Britain the judges give their services free, receiving only travelling expenses and hotel expenses for one night should this be required. Would-be judges have to undergo an intensive training programme before being considered for the position.

In Canada the first recorded show was held in Toronto in 1906, sponsored by the Royal Canadian Cat Club but it was not until 1961 that the Canadian Cat Association started registering cats for the first time in Canada.

There had been a great deal of interest in cats before this date and many cat clubs were already in existence but the cats were registered with one of the American organizations. World War II saw, as in Britain, almost the complete cessation of pedigree cat breeding and cat shows, but things started up again shortly after the war ended, with a number of breeders soon producing excellent kittens once again. Shows were held once more, with the Canadian National Cat Club sponsoring the important shows held at the Canadian National Exhibitions, an annual exhibition including shows for all kinds of animals. In 1968 the Canadian National Cat Club was disbanded and the Royal Canadian Cat Club took over the responsibility for the cat show at the exhibition.

Shows in Canada are run on similar lines to those in the United States and both countries participate freely in each other's cat activities. Cats from Canada may be shown in the United States, and *vice versa,* judges from both countries often officiating at the same show.

Interest in pedigree cats increases each year in Canada, with more and more clubs coming into being and more shows being held.

Generally the shows in the United States and Canada are not as large as those held in the British Isles but the distances to be travelled are very great and many exhibitors go by plane for quickness, although others travel many hundred of miles by car. The shows are usually two-day affairs.

For exhibitors showing cats both in Canada and in the United States there is the added excitement of winning one of the much-coveted awards, that of International Champion and International Grand Champion. A cat must be a Champion or a Grand Champion in each country to achieve this feat.

3 The Longhair Varieties Today

Ever since the first cat show was held in 1871 the cats with long coats have been general favourites. At first the noses were longish, the heads narrow, the ears large and the bodies rangey, but careful breeding over the years has brought about changes in the type and characteristics. These aristocratic cats, once knows as Angoras, then Persians and now in Britain officially as Longhairs, have broad heads, with small neat ears, short broad noses, big round eyes, and a frill framing the heads, cobby bodies on sturdy legs, long flowing coats and short full tails, without kinks. Some may have noses a little long, and eyes a little small. These faults only matter if the cat is to be shown or used for breeding, and most pet owners consider their own perfect.

The GCCF standard given below is for the Blues; other standards vary slightly according to the way the 100 points are allocated for the specific variety. Details of all the breeds and their standards may be purchased from the secretary of the GCCF.

Blue, breed no. 3

Coat: Any shade of blue allowable, sound and even in colour; free from markings, shadings or any white hairs. Fur long, thick and soft in texture. Frill full.

Head: Broad and round, with width between the ears. Face and nose short. Ears small and tufted. Cheeks well developed.

Eyes: Deep orange or copper; large round and full, without a trace of green.

Body: Cobby, and low on the legs.

Tail: Short and full, not tapering (a kink shall be considered a defect).

Orange-eyed White Longhair. This is Shirar Snowman, owned and bred by Mr and Mrs G. Martin.

Scale of points

Coat	20
Condition	10
Head	25
Eyes	20
Body	15
Tail	10
Total	**100**

By courtesy of the GCCF

Each variety in Britain is given a breed number, as follows:

Longhaired cats

1		Black
2		White (blue eyes)
2a		White (orange eyes)
2b		White (odd eyes)
3		Blue
4		Red Self
5		Cream
6		Smoke
6a		Blue Smoke
7		Silver Tabby
8		Brown Tabby
9		Red Tabby
10		Chinchilla
11		Tortoiseshell
12		Tortoiseshell and White
12a		Bi-Coloured
13		Blue-Cream
13b	(1)	Seal Colourpoint
13b	(2)	Blue Colourpoint
13b	(3)	Chocolate Colourpoint
13b	(4)	Lilac Colourpoint
13b	(5)	Red Colourpoint
13b	(6)	Tortie Colourpoint
13b	(7)	Cream Colourpoint
13b	(8)	Blue-cream Colourpoint
13b	(9)	Choc. Tortie Colourpoint
13b	(10)	Lilac Cream Colourpoint
13c		Birman
13d		Turkish
50b		Self Chocolate
50c		Self Lilac
51	(1)	Red Shell Cameo
51	(2)	Red Shaded Cameo
51	(3)	Red Smoke Cameo
51	(4)	Red Tortie Cameo
52	(1)	Cream Shell Cameo
52	(2)	Cream Shaded Cameo
52	(3)	Cream Smoke Cameo
52	(4)	Blue-Cream Cameo
53		Pewter

The would-be owner of a longhair kitten may find it bewildering to be faced with a choice of about 40 colour variations from which to choose. All are decorative, with great charm, usually with very good temperaments, very polite, and answering when spoken to; all make delightful pets.

Longhairs which are the same colour all over are referred to as Self. These include the Blacks, Whites, Blues, Creams, Reds, Chocolates and Lilacs.

The Blacks

These cats look glorious when adult and the lustrous raven-black coats are full and shining, contrasting well with the copper or deep orange eyes. At first sight a Black kitten may disappoint a would-be buyer as frequently the coat may be rusty brown with some white or grey hairs in the fur. As the kitten grows his appearance will change dramatically, and he will become a cat of which to be proud. If a Black is to be shown, he must be kept out of strong sunlight and damp, as these tend to give the fur a brownish tinge. Grooming is as for the other longhairs, but a beautiful sheen may be given to the coat by polishing with a soft silk scarf.

Sarasamsan Ragtime Girl, an Odd-eyed White Longhair — the different eye colours are clearly visible.

The Whites

The original Whites were the Angoras, the first longhairs seen in Europe; mostly they had blue eyes and were much prized. Cross-matings over the years have produced today's three varieties, the Blue-eyed, the Orange-eyed, and the Odd-eyed with one orange eye and one blue. They all have their own Open classes.

There is a slight element of risk in that the Blue-eyed variety may be deaf, as also may be the Odd-eyed on the blue-eyed side. Any white kitten should be carefully checked for deafness before buying. The kittens are pinkish when first born, but in a very short time the fur will grow into a beautiful white coat. They develop rapidly into delightful creatures, much in demand.

Grooming a White is not all that difficult, with talcum powder being sprinkled well into the fur and combed and brushed out. The corners of the eyes should be wiped so that there is no staining of the face to spoil the looks. Tails can be a problem as there may be some yellow staining, but it is possible to wash the tail with baby shampoo. Many exhibitors of Whites bath them a few days before the show, so that they have really sparkling coats on the day.

Blues

One of the most popular of the longhairs, and one which for years was regarded as being nearest to the required standard, with good typical longhair characteristics. All shades of blue are allowed, as long as the coat is the same colour all over. The eyes are deep orange or copper. As the type has been outstanding for many years, the Blues have been used to improve and produce other varieties, such as Orange-eyed Whites, Blacks, Creams, and the Colourpoints. They are also used in the breeding of Blue-creams. Mated to a Cream female, a Blue male may sire Blue-creams and Cream males: A Blue female mated to a Cream male may have Blue-creams and Blue males, while a Blue male mated to a Blue-cream may result in Blue females, Blue-creams, Blue males and Cream males. The newly born kittens have shadow tabby markings which rapidly disappear as the fur grows. They are very lively and intelligent. Blues seem to remain kitten-like all their lives even when as old as 15 years, they will rush around, chasing balls or small toys.

Red

This is a rare variety, but very striking with rich red flowing fur, with good type. They may be produced from Red Tabbies and are difficult to produce without tabby markings, which are a fault. It is often said that all Reds are males. This is untrue, as pure breeding on both sides can produce males and females in the litter. Reds are useful in breeding the female-only varieties, such as Torties and Torties and Whites, and have been used in the breeding programme for Cameos. As frequently longhaired kittens have tabby markings when first born, it may be difficult for some months to know if a kitten is a true Red Self.

Cream

A popular variety with full cream fur and deep copper eyes. By mating Blues and Creams together it is possible to produce Blues, Creams and Blue-creams in the litters. They are useful too as mates for Blacks, Torties and Torties and Whites. The type is usually very good. Faults are 'hot' colouring on the back and any tabby markings. The numbers are steadily increasing.

Smokes (Black and Blue)

Very striking varieties, with perfect specimens attracting much admiration, they are comparatively rare and most unusual. The Black has a white undercoat with the tips shading to black, and a black face with the frill and ear tufts silver. The Blue has a white undercoat with tips shading to blue, a blue face with silver tufts and frill. They are known as the 'cats of contrast' as it is not until they walk that a glimmer of white shows through the dark top coats. The eyes may be orange or copper in colour. At first it is exceedingly difficult for a novice breeder to know if the kittens are Smokes as they look self-coloured and it may be many weeks before the contrasts may be seen. These are really striking cats. Grooming is very important so that the undercoat is brushed up to show through the top coat.

Chocolate and Lilac Selfs

Two of the latest varieties to be given Championship status, although they originated from the planned breeding programme for Colourpoints many years ago. Fanciers were interested in them, but at first found them difficult to breed near the required type and with the correct eye colour, which should be deep orange or copper. The Chocolate should be a medium to dark chocolate brown and the Lilac a pinkish dove grey. White hairs in the fur or any markings are faults.

The Tabbies

There are three colours recognized, Brown, Red and Silver, all having the same markings — that is swirls on the cheeks, butterfly markings on the shoulders, pencil marks on the face, deep bands running down the side, and rings on the front of the legs and around the tail. In the Brown, the colour should be rich tawny

Opposite Grand Champion Chinchilla, Adelisa Romulus, with a good broad head and magnificent eye-colour. Owner Mrs Linda Taylor.

Shaded Silver, with the silver markings forming a mantle.

33

Taloola d'Artagnan, a Bi-colour with good division of the two colours. Owner and breeder Mrs J. Saunders.

sable, with black markings and the eyes may be hazel or copper. The Red should be a deep rich red colour, with darker red markings clearly defined. The eyes are a deep copper. In the Silver, the ground colour should be pale silver, with jet black markings. The eyes may be green or hazel. In the three varieties the markings are exceedingly difficult to see in the long fur, but for showing careful grooming can make the pattern show up.

The Brown Tabby kittens are well marked from birth, and are so attractive they are often bought as pets. The Red kittens are glowing little balls of fluff when young, and have tabby markings at birth. Sometimes these go and they may be Selfs. The Silvers' pattern is more easy to see, but here again it may be some weeks

before the true markings are apparent. Recently there has been a revival of interest in the Silver Tabbies, and now more are appearing at the shows. In the United States of America Blue and Cream Tabbies are also recognized.

Chinchillas

Thought to have originated from lightly marked Silver Tabbies, this variety is often referred to as the most glamorous of the longhairs. The pure white coat should be delicately tipped with black and from the distance has a sparkling silver appearance. The large emerald or blue-green eyes, and the brick-red tip to the nose add to the cat's striking appearance. Chinchillas are frequently used in

The heavy tipping should take the form of a mantle. The eyes should be green or blue-green.

Tortoiseshells and Tortoiseshells and Whites (Calicos)

Both these varieties are usually female only, with the occasional male that may be produced proving sterile. The Torties have a patched coat of cream, red and black, the Torties and Whites having the black, red and cream patches interspersed with white. The faces and even the ears should be broken, with small patches. Torties are difficult to produce to order, but can result from cross-matings between Blacks, Creams, Red Selfs and Blue-creams. The type is usually good, and the eyes may be orange or copper. The Torties and Whites too were very

Note the good blue eyes in this study of a Sealpoint Colourpoint, Nickel Estee. Owner and breeder Mrs L. Saunders.

advertising, and their popularity and the numbers bred have greatly increased over the years. When first born, the kittens are very dark, and frequently are a great disappointment to a novice breeder, but as the coat grows it gradually lightens, and often the darkest kitten becomes a prize-winning adult. The type is as for other longhairs, but sometimes the heads are not so broad nor the noses so short.

Shaded Silvers

These may be seen at shows in some countries, but they are not yet recognized in Britain. The distinguishing feature is that the coat is more heavily tipped than that of the Chinchillas, although they may be born in the same litter.

Gr Ch Mister Jubilee: a
Blue Colourpoint.
Owner Miss Monika
Forster; breeder Mrs
Pat Rawlins.

Opposite Grand
Premier Sealpoint
Birman, Strathdean
Saroki Chio. Owner
and breeder Mrs T.
Cole.

difficult to breed until a certain breeding
programme was evolved using Bi-Colour males
with specific breeding. Once known as the
'Chintz' cats in Britain, they are referred to as
'Calicos' in the United States of America. There
is always a ready demand for both varieties.
Used for breeding, they may produce a variety
of different coloured kittens, very lively and all
most attractive.

Bi-Colours

In the early days of the Cat Fancy, cats with two-
coloured coats were shown, but these were
usually shorthairs. A few longhairs did appear
but were invariably neutered as pets. As
mentioned earlier, it was then found that Bi-
Colours, if correctly bred, could be used to
breed the Torties and Whites. At first the
standard given was too exacting and few did

well at the shows. This was amended and their popularity grew, and they have been Best in Show. The standard says that any solid colour and white is allowed, but tabby markings are a fault. The eyes may be deep orange or copper.

Blue-creams

This is a female-only variety, with any males proving sterile. Produced from cross-matings with Blues and Creams, and sometimes appearing in Tortie litters, the coat is unusual in that the two pastel colours should be softly intermingled. When first bred in Britain, the coats were very patched and they were often referred to as Blue Torties. In the United States the standard calls for the coats to be patched, not intermingled. The cross-breeding produces kittens with good type, sturdy and healthy, and much liked for breeding. The classes at the shows are invariably well filled.

Colourpoints and Himalayans

These are exciting varieties in that they were man-made many years ago when a fancier planned a careful breeding programme starting with a Siamese and a Blue Longhair, which ultimately resulted in the Colourpoints. In the United States a similar programme produced the much-admired Himalayans. Both varieties have the light-coloured bodies and the contrasting points colouring with good longhair type. There is no similarity in shape to the slinky Siamese apart from the points and the blue eyes.

It is both expensive and difficult to start to produce a new variety as in the early days of such a programme many kittens are of little use, not conforming with the variety planned. These have to be given away as neutered pets.

The colour of the body depends on the points colour, e.g. Seal points with cream body, and Blue points with glacial white body. The

large round eyes should be bright and decidedly blue. By cross-breeding the Colourpoints are now bred in ten point colours (see page 27) and are immensely popular. The kittens are born with creamish fur, with the points developing during the first few weeks. They are energetic at an early age, very inquisitive, and most affectionate.

Birmans

These longhaired cats should not be confused with the shorthaired Burmese. Birmans are said to have originated in the temples of Burma and were introduced into France in the 1920s, where they are known as the Sacred Cats of Burma. The standard differs from other longhairs as the heads are not so broad; the ears are medium in size, there is no stop to the noses, and the coats are not so luxuriant. They have the Siamese coat pattern, i.e. light bodies with contrasting points, but with the most distinguishing feature of white paws: the front points like little white gloves; and on the back paws pure white gauntlets covering the entire paws and tapering up the backs to points. The eyes are blue. They have become very popular both as pets and at the shows. Two variations are recognized, the Seal, with pale beige, slightly golden body colouring and dark brown points, and the Blue with body bluish-white, cold in tone, and blue-grey points. It is also possible to breed other point colours.

The Turkish

Similar in type to the original Angoras, to which they must have been related, these cats were introduced into Britain some years ago direct from the Van area of Turkey. Compared with most other longhaired varieties, the heads are wedge-shaped rather than round, the ears large, and the noses long. The bodies too are longish and the tails medium length. The eyes are light amber colour. Turkish cats differ from the original Angoras in that although the long silky fur is also chalk-white, they have auburn markings on the face, and auburn tails with faint rings. Although not in the standard some small auburn markings elsewhere are permitted. In hot weather they seem to shed their coats, sometimes appearing almost shorthaired. In Turkey they are known to swim in warm pools and shallow rivers.

The kittens, even when newly born, have the distinct auburn markings. They develop early, are highly intelligent and make decorative pets, devoted to their owners.

From Britain they have been sent all over the world, but the numbers at British shows are not increasing greatly.

Cameos

Known in the United States for many years, these cats are being produced by selective breeding in Britain and now have provisional standards. They are bred both in Red and Cream, with four variations in each colour. The undercoats are white, with tippings and shadings of red and cream. The Red variations are as follows: the Shell is lightly tipped with rose pink; the Shaded with red shading giving the effect of a red mantle; the Smoke with red shading on the sides and face and red mask and feet; the Tortie with black, red and cream tipping, broken into patches. In the Cream, there is the Shell, the Shaded and the Smoke, with cream replacing the red, and also a Blue-cream Cameo with blue and cream intermingled tipping. The eyes in all variations to be orange or copper. The type is for other longhairs, with broad head, small ears and so on. The cross-breeding has produced very pretty cats with very good type, very attractive in appearance.

With their distinctive auburn markings, a Turkish mother and her kitten: Erevan Kayisi, and Erevan Benim. Owner and breeder Mrs Sims.

Pewter

This variety has a provisional standard and can be shown only in the Assessment classes. The standard is similar to that of the Shaded Silvers, with white undercoat shaded with black, giving the impression of a mantle. Type is as for other longhairs, and the eye colour orange or copper with a black rim. At first they were produced by the mating of Chinchillas to Blues, and later to Blacks. It was decided that the name Pewter should be used, as it would not be connected with Chinchillas or Shaded Silvers, both of which should have sea-green or emerald eyes.

Having a provisional standard means that breeders should show as many as possible in the Assessment classes gaining merit certificates, as these and the numbers being bred are taken into consideration when an application is made for a full recognized standard which would mean Championship status.

Cream Shaded Cameo, Snowzetta Polperro, with white undercoat and cream tips. Owner and breeder Mrs N. Boyle.

Turkish Angoras

These are bred in the United States and should have the type of the original Angoras, that is the heads should be smallish, the ears long and pointed, the eyes almond shaped. The body should be longish, and the tail should be long and tapering, the silky coat of medium length. There are now a number of coat colourings, although the White still seems to be the favourite.

Peke-faced

There is no British standard for this variety which is similar to the Red Tabbies and Red Selfs, except for the heads. These should be as much like those of the Pekingese dogs as possible. The noses are snub and indented between the eyes and the muzzles wrinkled. The brilliant copper or deep orange eyes are very large and round. They carry very full rich red coats. In Britain they would be referred to as 'over-typed', as it is feared that the cats might have breathing problems with such short noses. They can appear in litters from normal Reds.

Golden Persians or Golden Chinchillas

These are now appearing in Britain from certain strains of Chinchillas. They do not yet have a Provisional standard but may be seen at the shows on exhibition. When first born they look very much like miniature Brown Tabbies but as the coats clear, most of the tabby markings vanish, leaving kittens with creamish fur, tipped with dark brown giving a golden effect. When adult, the back, flanks, head, ears and tail should be lightly tipped with dark brown, the nose tip brick-red and the eyes emerald or blue-green.

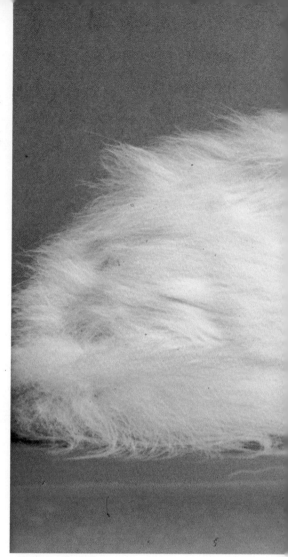

Maine Coon

These cats originated in Maine in the United States over 100 years ago and were thought to have resulted from longhaired cats, brought in by sailors and merchants, intermating with the resident shorthairs. Massive, strong and healthy, the Maine Coons have longish fur, but not so luxuriant as those of the Persians. At first

Norwegian Forest Cat

mostly Brown Tabbies with some white, their popularity has rapidly spread, and now all colours and coat patterns are permitted. They are not recognized in Britain. The name 'Coon' was given as it was once thought they were bred by cats and raccoons mating, but this is not possible.

Similar in appearance and having very much the same history as the Maine Coon, these cats have been known in Norway for several centuries. All colours and coat patterns are allowed, but there is usually some white on the paws and chest.

The correct shadings are just appearing in this Pewter kitten, Chirunga Silver Mist. Owner and breeder Mrs Kayes.

Other varieties

Classified under the Shorthairs, but having fairly long fur, are the **Balinese** or longhaired Siamese, which originated by a natural mutation in Siamese litters. The coats are light with contrasting points colouring and the tails long and fluffy. The almond-shaped eyes are blue. Also classified under the Shorthairs are the **Somalis**, long-coated Abyssinians. The coats are fairly long, with each hair banded with black in the Usual, and chocolate in the Sorrel. The eyes should be hazel, amber or green.

These varieties are judged only by Shorthair judges.

4 The Longhairs as Pets: Acquisition and Care

You may be thinking of having a longhair kitten as a pet and have seen or read about the many delightful varieties there are available. Before even considering any particular one, it is as well to consider the advantages and the dis-advantages of owning such a pet.

It should be remembered that a 12 week-old adorable bundle of fluff will rapidly grow into an equally lovable but very large cat that will need daily grooming to keep that immaculate look; and which will certainly live a long life, maybe as long as 20 years given care, affection and good mixed feeding. He will have to be fed two or three times a day, and if there is no garden, will need the litter tray changed constantly. When holiday time comes around arrangements will have to be made for his welfare. The development of his character will depend very much on the attention and the time you give to him when young. In return for this you will have a charming pet that will give you constant companionship and affection, and be a most decorative addition to your home.

Because of their short noses and flat faces, which tend to give the longhairs an aloof and aristocratic look, they are sometimes thought to be bad-tempered. This is not true; generally they have quieter temperaments and are less noisy than some of the shorthaired varieties. If you are away from home all day it is really better not to have a young kitten, but you could consider taking on an older cat needing a home, from one of the animal welfare societies.

A happy solution is to buy two kittens which will be companions for one another and to try to come home at mid-day to feed them, or to get a neighbour to come in to see that everything is all right.

If you buy two kittens to grow up together, and they are different sexes, they should be neutered at the age recommended by the vet, otherwise you may become a breeder unwittingly. When you buy a kitten as a pet it does not really matter about the sex, as it will be advisable to have it neutered in any case. If a male is allowed freedom, when old enough he will travel for miles seeking likely females, and may return with torn ears and bleeding wounds, having been involved in fights with other males. He will undoubtedly make the house smell with his strong tom-cat odours, even spraying indoors. A female will come into season as soon as she is developed enough and will need to be constantly watched to see that she does not get out and get mated with the local Romeo. Some female longhairs are far from noisy when in season but a few may really howl and even upset the neighbours, as well as attracting any roving male that may be around.

The best age for neutering will depend on the kitten's development, and the vet will advise on this. Generally 3½ months for a male and 4½ months for a female will be considered the right age, although in the USA some think that the time after the first heat is the best for a female and about nine months for a male. Anaesthetics are given for the operations

Some things are better done in private.

whatever the age. It will be a little more serious for a female than a male, as she will have a stitch or two and will need a few days' nursing.

Obviously a garden is best for a cat to use as a toilet, but cats can live happily in a flat, using toilet trays and with pots of grass to chew, to prevent fur balls. A wired-in balcony would make an ideal sun-bathing spot.

Once having decided which variety of longhaired kitten you would like, it is not always easy to find one. The best plan is to visit a cat show, see the different kinds, talk to the breeders and maybe order a kitten. It is not advisable to buy one straight from a show, as even if the kitten is inoculated against feline infectious enteritis (and it must have been to be allowed in the show), there are still other illnesses which can be picked up and which

may not be apparent for a few days. There are in Britain two useful periodicals: *Cats,* which comes out weekly, and *Cat World,* a monthly. These carry advertisements for kittens, and may be ordered through a newsagent.

If possible visit the breeder's house and see the way the animals are kept. If given the choice of a litter, choose a lively and energetic kitten, with big bright eyes, clean ears, and fur that stands away from the body, whose little tail is held upright, with no signs of diarrhoea underneath. The kitten should be sturdy and well-fed, with fur well-groomed and with no signs of flea dirts. He should be at least 12 weeks old, and house-trained.

Collect the kitten in a suitable container, as it is inadvisable to have a young kitten on the lap when taking it in a car. Some take it all quite calmly but others may panic, missing the mother and usual surroundings. Some may dribble and others may mew all the time, but in closed containers with warm blankets, they may not notice the unaccustomed motion of the car so much; they may even settle down and sleep until arriving in the new home.

At home have ready a cosy bed. You may buy one of those especially made for kittens but a small cardboard box with newspaper and a blanket is ideal to begin with. This could be under a cupboard or a table in a corner where the kitten will feel secure and can hide if scared. Place the sanitary tray on newspaper near the bed at first, using the litter recommended by the breeder. Peat can be used but this does get scattered around, and unless changed constantly earth does get very muddy.

Put the kitten in one room at first, making sure that all the windows and doors are closed and the chimney blocked, or closely guarded if there is an open fire. It may never have seen a fire in its short life and will not appreciate the danger. Allow the kitten plenty of time to inspect the new home and do not keep picking it up or allowing young children to do so. The young bones are very fragile and are easily broken or injured if the kitten is squeezed or dropped. Grooming should be a daily routine. You will need a soft brush, a wide-toothed comb and a narrow pronged one to remove dirt and the possible odd flea.

It will be an easy task at first to groom the small fluffy kitten, but a grown cat with a very full coat will be different matter, needing at least 20 minutes each day, or even two such sessions during the spring and autumn when the coat is being shed and knots up quickly. Some cats do not take kindly to being brushed and combed, especially on the stomach. If this is the case, 'little and often' is the rule. Have ready a little cotton wool to wipe the corners of the eyes, and inside the ears to remove any dust that may collect. Comb through the coat with the wide toothed comb and brush well. The fur around the head should be brushed up to form a frame for the face. This is known as the frill. With a light coat, a little baby talcum powder sprinkled in the fur and brushed out thoroughly will remove any grease.

Finding a suitable name can be difficult. If the kitten is already registered it will have a pedigree with its name on it. This will bear the breeder's cattery name, that is a prefix which

Blue-cream Longhair. This is Lafrebella Julie. Owner Mrs I. Harding; breeder Mrs I. Bangs.

may only be used by him/her, for example 'Bluestar', and then a name which could be 'Playboy' for a male or 'Honey' for a female. If you do not like the given name, you can always give the kitten a pet name to which in a day or two he will answer readily. If the kitten is not already registered the breeder may be able to use the name you suggest with his/her prefix. The kitten must be transferred officially to you and this is done by completing the form that the breeder will give you and sending it with the appropriate fee to the secretary of the registering body. If you are going to show the kitten, it must have been transferred to you at least three weeks before the show day.

The kitten will require four small meals a day, which should follow the diet sheet given you by the breeder. This should be kept to for the first few weeks, and any new item introduced a little at a time and the effect noted. A change of home may cause a slight digestive upset resulting in diarrhoea or constipation. In the case of diarrhoea, cut down on the liquids and sprinkle on the food a little kaolin, easily obtained from the chemist. In the case of constipation serve food a little moister with a teaspoonful of vegetable oil. The diet may include scraped raw beef, cooked meat such as lamb, rabbit, chicken, a little liver or heart, with a few cornflakes or brown bread mixed with it for roughage. Boned, cooked white fish may be included but not all cats are fish lovers. It is important to give a mixed diet and too much fish can cause eczema. There are excellent canned foods on the market, which are very good when the kitten is older, and there is also one made particularly for kittens. Not all kittens can take cow's milk as it may cause looseness, but others drink it with no ill-effects; but really evaporated milk is better. Porridge, rice pudding or one of the prepared baby canned meals are also good. A few vegetables may also be given. A raw beef bone may be liked and

does help teething, but cooked bones of any kind should not be included, as they may splinter and cause internal damage.

Kittens' stomachs are very small, and about a tablespoonful each of the four meals should be sufficient, with the amounts being increased as the kitten grows. At about six months the meals may be cut down to three and at about a year old, to two. It is as well to give as varied a diet as possible, as not only will it provide all that is necessary for the kitten to grow up strong and healthy, but it will also ensure that it will not be too fussy if a certain item cannot be obtained. There should always be clean water on the floor for drinking. This is essential, for milk is a food not a drink. The kitten should always have access to grass for chewing which acts as an emetic and helps to prevent fur ball. A weekly dose of a teaspoonful of liquid paraffin or vegetable oil will also be helpful for this, as well as daily grooming to remove any loose hairs. If there are other pets, say another cat or a dog, introduce them slowly, and never leave them alone together for the first week or so, thereafter they should have begun to accept one another. Feed the pets separately and make an extra fuss of the resident animals, so that they are not jealous. Give plenty of toys, such as toy mice and small balls, so that the kitten gets plenty of exercise. After the grooming session try to play with the kitten, giving it special attention. This will make it look forward to being groomed.

If your kitten was not inoculated against feline infectious enteritis before you bought it this should be done as soon as it has settled down and before it comes into contact with other cats. FIE, as it is known, is a killer illness. Once it is contracted there is little hope of recovery, but inoculation does give almost 100 per cent immunity. The symptoms are varied, with low temperature, vomiting, deterioration in general condition, lassitude, and perhaps

diarrhoea. It is vital that the vet be called in at once, as death can follow in a few hours. If this does happen another kitten should not be brought into the house for at least six months. No cat or kitten may now be exhibited at any cat show unless it has a current vaccination certificate. Cat flu (also known as feline viral rhinotracheitis, or FVR) is a disease which affects the nasal passages. It is very contagious and can be picked up at any time and early veterinary treatment is essential. At first it may be suspected that the cat has just caught cold, as there may be a high temperature and running nose and eyes, with coughing and sneezing. The cat may become listless and lose its appetite. Good nursing is essential as is an even temperature. There are several vaccinations available against cat flu, but as there are a number of different viruses, complete immunity can never be guaranteed.

Another worrying illness which has only comparatively recently been recognized is feline infectious leukaemia (FCLV) which affects the condition of the blood. The symptoms are various, but may mean loss of appetite, wasting, and, eventually, collapse. There is no known cure at the moment. In the main it seems to attack a number of cats kept in close proximity. Many breeders have their cats regularly tested to ensure that they are free. Should your cat seem off-colour it is advisable to consult a vet straight away.

It is always important to ensure that your cat is flea-free, as fleas can be responsible for worms, skin diseases, and anaemia. Any animal can pick up the occasional flea, but daily grooming and the use of a flea comb to catch them and sprays or powders recommended by the vet should keep these pests at bay. Fleas do not breed on the cat but may do so in the bedding and other places where the cat likes to sleep.

Cats which live in the country may pick up ticks, which are rather horrible. Greyish-blue in appearance, they hang on to the cat's skin by the head, sucking the blood until bloated to the size of a pea. Flea powders are useless, and each tick must be first of all dabbed with surgical spirit, and then removed without pulling, as removal may otherwise leave the head embedded in the cat's body, causing a sore. The cat's skin should be dabbed with a mild disinfectant afterwards. If not removed, ticks can cause anaemia.

Lice are sometimes found on cats. These are pale grey and flat. They attach themselves to the cat, laying their eggs, referred to as nits, in the coat, causing the cat to keep scratching. Treatment is the same as for fleas, but may need to be repeated weekly until all trace of them has gone. They can be picked off with tweezers.

Tapeworms can be caused by fleas or if a cat kills and eats rats and mice. Segmented and flat, they may be seen looking like flat, dry grains of rice in the fur under the tail and as segments in the motions. The head attaches itself to the intestine, and the body can grow up to several feet in length. Tapeworms cause rapid loss of condition, irritation, and swollen stomachs. Modern treatment ordered by the vet will easily clear up the condition, but it should be repeated in a few weeks to ensure that the tapeworm has gone completely.

Roundworms may be seen in the motions, looking like thin spaghetti, and can vary from half-an-inch to three inches in length. They affect kittens and cats, kittens in particular, causing the fur to look spiky and the tummy swollen, and the haws may be up in the corners of the eyes. It is important that you get correct medicine from your vet, as indiscriminate worming has been the death of many a young kitten. The vet will probably recommend piperazine which has been used safely for many years. A second dose should be given after two weeks to ensure that no larvae have been left.

If a cat or kitten keeps shaking its head and

The Somali (this is Harvey Wallbanger) resembles an Abyssinian with a longer coat — it is one of the 'Foreign' varieties. Owner Miss Jacqui Murphy; breeders the Somali Breeders' Society.

Dogs and cats become
excellent companions
if brought up together.
This Balthazar
Chinchilla kitten is
owned and bred by
Mrs C. Philbrick.

scratching the ears, examine the ears carefully. There may be a nasty smell and a slight discharge which is caused by ear mites. Very tiny, they are not easy to see without a magnifying glass. Usually referred to by the layman as canker, they need specific treatment by a vet. If the condition is very bad he may wash the ear out and recommend ear drops to be given daily. If there are other animals in the household, their ears should be looked at as well as the mites can easily be passed from one animal to another.

There are several skin diseases which cats may get. These include eczema, which is not contagious, and can take various forms. It may be caused by an allergy, for example, to excessive fish or even milk. Ringworm is very contagious, and can be passed on to humans by a cat or vice versa. It can be picked up from infected rats or mice. Bald roundish patches may be seen in the fur. The animal should be isolated and handled with rubber gloves, and an overall worn when treatment is administered. The cat's bedding and anything he sleeps on should be replaced. Modern treatment, which can only be prescribed by a vet, should be started as soon as possible.

Longhaired cats will sometimes vomit a small sausage-shaped wad of fur, which is referred to as furball or hairball. This may happen after chewing grass, which is a natural emetic, and should always be available. Daily grooming to remove the old hairs, which otherwise the cat would lick down when washing, and a weekly dose of corn or similar oil or liquid paraffin should prevent the accumulation of fur inside; it could otherwise form a solid mass which would cause problems.

Rabies is a terrifying disease, invariably fatal, affecting both humans and animals. It is known in many parts of the world but fortunately, due to strict quarantine laws, not in Britain. At any time some person could smuggle in an animal

In Britain the judges and stewards go to the cat's pen to carry out the judging.

which may later develop rabies and cause wide-spread alarm and many deaths. This could mean wholesale slaughter of wildlife over a large area.

Any cat imported into Britain must go into quarantine for six months. On arrival the animal is collected by a Ministry of Agriculture approved carrier and taken to a quarantine cattery. An inoculation against rabies is given on admission and another just before leaving. Cats entering some other countries may have to

have a rabies injection and have a certificate to that effect before being allowed to enter. It is essential to check on the local regulations. Cats that do live in countries where rabies is known should have inoculations and regular boosters.

The majority of longhaired cats and kittens are extremely healthy, living long happy lives, and rarely needing the vet's services, but it should be remembered that booster inoculations are given for feline infectious enteritis.

5 Breeding

If considering going in for breeding, as a beginner you should spend plenty of time visiting shows, speaking to the exhibitors, walking around the hall and looking at the kittens. You should buy a catalogue and make a note of the prizewinners and others in the same class and see if you agree with the judges' choice. This may well help you to make up your mind as to which variety you would like to breed. Try to make an appointment to go to a breeder's house and see the animals there. Do not rush into buying a kitten direct from a show, as there is always the risk of some infection. If you do see a kitten that you like when visiting the house, be quite honest about the fact that you intend to breed from any kitten that you are likely to buy. It is unfair to make out that you are just looking for a pet, although your kitten will probably also be treated as your pet. The price for a pet kitten and one with good future breeding potential can vary considerably. It is better to buy a kitten as near to the recognized standard as possible, and the best you can afford. Ask the breeder to tell you the good and bad points of a kitten, particularly if you intend to show. If possible ask to see the mother, and the male if he is there as well, so you will have an idea of what the adult cat will be like. Ask to see the pedigree. Even if full of Champions it will probably mean little to you, but a good pedigree does show that the kitten has been bred from good stock, and may well eventually produce a future Champion, even if she never becomes a Champion herself.

It is better to start with a female only and to send her to stud when old enough. It is not practical to buy a male and a female and hope that kittens will arrive in due course. Males and females mature at different ages, and a male will need more than one female to keep him happy. You must look on breeding as a pleasant hobby for it will certainly not be a paying one, with the cost of feeding, stud fees, injections and possibly other veterinary bills. If you do get 'bitten' with the 'breeding bug' you will find that three or four well-kept and loved females living as house pets will do better than large numbers kept in an outside cattery.

The age at which your female will start calling is very difficult to predict. Some come into season (that is, calling or on heat) when only five months old, and others at seven or eight months, or as late as a year. An average age for the longhairs is about six months, but at that age she will not be developed enough to be mated. Ten months is young enough for mating, and only then if it is her second call at least. It may be difficult to know when she is calling, as not all longhairs are noisy, but some of them certainly let everybody know. The first sign is usually excessive friendliness, with the cat following her owner around, probably letting out little plaintive mews, rubbing against her owner's legs, then rolling on the ground and eventually padding up and down on the floor with the back legs. She may start really yelling, so much so that the alarmed owner may think that she is in terrible pain. A

This Silver Tabby Longhair shows the correct coat markings. — Ch Santiago Silver Sosa. Owner Mrs V. Chard; breeder Mrs J. Massie.

close examination under the tail will show that the vulva is swollen, and there is a slight discharge. This may not be noticed if a cat is always washing herself. The length of the call may vary considerably from cat to cat and can be from about two or three days up to about ten. The time between the calls varies too, some cats calling every month, some every two or three months, and others only once a year. A careful watch will have to be kept on the queen (as she is called when old enough to be mated), as not only may she use every endeavour to get out, but hopeful males may be waiting outside making determined efforts to get in!

Choosing the stud, for which an appointment should be made well in advance, is very important. Not only should he be a very good example of the variety, correcting any faults which the female may have, and looking well fed and well groomed, but the conditions under which he is kept should also be seen if possible. Ask to see the actual house your cat will be put in to get to know the male. The stud fee will have to be paid in advance when the female goes there. If by any chance the mating does not take, and no kittens result, a second mating may be given later, but this is not obligatory. The cat must have had a feline infectious enteritis certificate and some stud owners also insist on a certificate certifying that she is free of feline infectious leukaemia. The stud fee will vary according to the male's status. For a Champion it may well be high and for a Grand Champion higher still. Cats may be sent by train but if possible it is better to take the queen yourself. If sent by train she should be in an adequate-sized basket or box, quite escape-proof. If the container is a basket and the weather is cold, put brown paper half-way up outside to prevent chills. Put a warm blanket in for her to sit on. Notify the stud owner directly she starts to call and send the cat on the second day, arranging with the stud owner the time of

arrival, so that the cat will not be kept waiting on a draughty station. Try to avoid a change of trains. When you have put her on the train, telephone to say that she is on her way. Mark the basket with the name of the stud owner and the station to which the cat is going, and put in large letters 'To be collected'.

Your cat will be there at least three days, or longer, and then you will have to collect her or arrange for her return by train. Once home again she must be well guarded and kept

indoors until the calling has stopped, which may be a week or more. If allowed out beforehand she may meet another male and a dual mating could happen, with kittens by both the stud and the rogue male being born in the same litter. This is a pity but would in no way affect her future breeding. Before going to stud she should have been wormed out, and naturally she should be flea-free. Do not treat her as an invalid on her return; allow her to exercize and give a good mixed diet. At about

the sixth week give an extra mid-day milk feed. After three weeks the first signs of a successful mating may be seen with the nipples turning pink. About the fifth or sixth week a definite swelling of the sides may be noticed. The period for gestation is about 65 days, but may vary by a day or two. A few weeks before the kittens are due prepare a kittening box, which could be of tough cardboard, with the bottom covered with plenty of newspaper, which she may well shred up, almost making a nest. It is

cats manage everything on their own, washing the kittens and cleaning up, but should she seem to be in distress, straining for some time with nothing happening, it is as well to telephone the vet. In any case, for a first litter it is well to notify your vet of the approximate date in case his help is required, although this rarely happens.

The kittens are born one at a time in separate transparent sacs which should be broken by the mother by tearing with her teeth, releasing the kitten which she will start washing immediately. If she does not tear the sac this can be done quite easily and gently by tearing around the head with a finger nail. They are born attached by the umbilical cord to the placenta or afterbirth. The mother bites through the cord and usually eats the placenta. There should be one for each kitten. If she does not eat it and the cord is still attached, cut with sterilised scissors about 1½ inches from the navel, and dispose of the placenta. The kitten should start breathing and giving a little mew as she washes it. Sometimes the kittens arrive very quickly and it is as well to have a wrapped hot water bottle in a small box standing by to put the first ones born on while she is coping with the next birth. Be careful not to put the kittens on to a too-hot, unprotected bottle. The kittens are born blind but in a matter of minutes make their way to the nipples by instinct and start suckling, padding away with their paws which helps to stimulate the flow of milk. When it appears that there are no more kittens, remove the newspapers, which may be dampened and stained, and without disturbing the mother too much, put her in the blanket, with all the kittens under her. Give her a warm drink and a light meal if she will take it, and leave the little family to settle down quietly.

Longhairs are not so prolific breeders as some shorthairs, with four kittens being about the average, but six or seven can occur. Two litters a year is enough and many breeders allow only one.

Tortoiseshell and Whites are another female-only variety: here is Sarasamsan Foxfire, with striking, bright colouring. Owner and breeder Mrs S. Corris.

better to put in a thick blanket after the kittens are born. To make things easier for the female nearer the date of the birth clip the fur away from around the nipples, being careful not to nip her, to make suckling easier, and from around the vulva to make the births cleaner. As kittening time grows nearer she will have to be watched to ensure that she does have the kittens in the box provided and not in your bed or in a drawer full of clean linen. She may well be restless, wanting her owner around, and there may be signs of milk in the nipples. The first sign that the kittens are imminent may be a kind of bubble protruding from her rear. Most

If you wish to know the sex of the kittens this may be established a day or two after the birth, before the fur grows too much, if the mother has no objection to having her kittens handled. Handle the kittens with care as they are only about the size of mice. In the female will be seen a small slit, which is the entrance to the vagina, close to the anus under the tail, while the male has a circular anus near the base of the tail, with rudimentary testicles about half an inch away. If the male and female are held close together the difference may be clearly seen. If the mother appears to have plenty of milk, with the kittens suckling contentedly and sleeping most of the time, they will need little attention for the first week or two. If one seems under-sized after a day or two he should be examined carefully to see that everything is normal, and if it is the rest of the litter can be taken away while he has an extra feed, or supplementary feeding may be given in a tiny feeding bottle, using evaporated milk or a baby food. The eyes should open when about twelve days old, but should there be a slight discharge, smear the lids with a little Vaseline. Should they look swollen and fail to open consult your vet. The mother cat should be given extra meals and milky drinks whilst feeding her family.

When three weeks old weaning may start with a few drops of baby food in a small egg spoon. One kitten may well refuse to show any interest while another will try to lick it up straight away. About a week later the kittens may be able to lap from small saucers, having a

A Cream Longhair stud with excellent type — this is Barwell Timothy. Owner Mrs Pullen.

Lamplighters Leola, a blue-and-white Bi-colour, owned and bred by Mrs O'Donohughe.

teaspoonful each. Gradually baby cereal may be added, and a few drops of milk of magnesia to aid digestion, and two meals given a day. At five weeks, scraped raw beef, minced chicken or rabbit, boned and mashed cooked white fish, and baby foods may be given. Do not over do it, for the mother will still be feeding them as well. Never rush the weaning, as the supply of mother's milk should be allowed to reduce gradually, otherwise she may get an abcess through a blockage. She should be willing to leave the kittens for a while and her milky feeds should be stopped and water given to drink, which should have been there for her all the time. By the age of eight to nine weeks the kittens should be completely weaned and used to a variety of foods, having four to five small meals a day.

When the kittens are about three weeks old, put down a small litter tray. Having been shown it once or twice kittens seem to toilet train themselves, but the tray must be kept clean and changed frequently.

They should be ready to be sold when about twelve weeks old, but a week or two before this it may be as well to advertise them in *Cats* or local newspapers. If you are interested in showing and wish to become known as a breeder, you may care to exhibit one of the best when at least thirteen weeks old. Wins at shows may well bring in orders for any future kittens.

Comparatively few fanciers put a male at public stud these days, although there are some very nice ones around. If thinking of having a stud it will have to be really outstanding if you intend to have visiting queens as well as using him for your own females. It should be remembered too that it will almost certainly be necessary to provide a house and large run for him in the garden, well away from neighbours who will complain about the noises that may come from there. Before taking on a stud, it is as well to go to a local library and read as much as possible about keeping a male and the housing it will need. It is not an easy way to make money. Hours will be spent in a stud house as all matings should be supervised to ensure that they have taken place. Some queens can be very difficult although some are very easy. The first mating for a young stud cat should be with an experienced queen.

The points colouring is just appearing in these Colourpoint kittens, from Mrs P. Pye's Venn cattery.

6 Cat Clubs and the Cat Fancy

The clubs are the lifelines of the Cat Fancy. If there were no clubs there could not be a pedigree Cat Fancy, as the Governing Council of the Cat Fancy is composed of delegates from all the affiliated clubs in Britain.

To become affiliated a club must have its rules and accounts approved by the Council, and have a certain number of members. Once affiliation has been granted and the appropriate fees paid, a club may send the member elected at the annual general meeting as their delegate to the council's quarterly meeting. The delegate may speak on behalf of the club on any specific item that it has put forward to go on the agenda and which was felt by its members to be for the good of a breed or breeds, or for the club, or for the Cat Fancy generally. The role of the GCCF is described in more detail on page 20.

There are dozens of clubs throughout the British Isles. Some are breed clubs, that is they look after the interests of breeders of specific varieties. There are also all-breed and area clubs, such as the National Cat Club, the Midland Cat Club, the Bedford Cat Club and many others. These clubs have members who are interested in many varieties, and usually run quite large Championship shows. The breed clubs may cater for one or several individual varieties, and the longhair fanciers have a choice of a number. They include affiliated and non-affiliated clubs:

Angora Cat Club
Birman Cat Club
Black & White Cat Club
Black, Red Self & Tortoiseshell Cat Club
Blue Persian Cat Club
Cameo Pewter & Smoke Cat Society
Capital Longhair Cat Association (all longhairs)
Celtic Longhair Cat Society (all longhairs)
Chinchilla, Silver Tabby & Smoke Cat Society
Chocolate & Lilac Longhairs
Chocolate & Lilac Persian Cat Society
Colourpoint Cat Club
Colourpoint, Rex-coated & AOV Cat Club
East Anglian Persian Cat Society (all longhairs)
Longhair Cream & Blue Cream Cat Association
Longhair Cat Club (all longhairs)
North of Britain Long-hair Cat Club (all longhairs)
RCT Society (Red, Cream and Tortie and other varieties)
6 and 6a Smoke Society
Tabby Cat Club
Tortie & White & Bi-Colour Cat Club
United Chinchilla Association
White Persian Cat Club

When a club has been in existence for a number of years, and has satisfied the GCCF that it has the requisite number of members and is financially strong, it may apply to hold an Exemption Show. This is a small show where no championship certificates are given, and there are comparatively few classes, but the procedure is much the same as for the larger shows. An Exemption Show gives a novice exhibitor an excellent opportunity to learn all

about showing and to see how an animal behaves when being handled by the judges and stewards. There may be opportunities too to talk to the judges and to ask them about the standard of the exhibit, and to know whether it is suitable for future showing and possibly breeding. When a club has held several Exemption Shows and all has gone well, it may

apply to hold a Sanction Show, which is bigger and is run on the same lines exactly as a Championship Show, but again no challenge certificates are given; in other respects it is really a rehearsal for a Championship Show. Several such shows must be organized by the club, and everything must have been satisfactory before a club will be granted

Red Colourpoint with a good mask and points — Ch Nickel Topas, owned and bred by Mrs L. Saunders.

One of the newest varieties, the Self Lilac Longhair with its delicate colouring. The photograph shows Trefleur Lilac Limerick. Owner Miss S.L. Booth; breeder Miss E. Eade.

Below Red Shaded Cameo; shown here is Holdenhurst Pink Floyd. Owner and breeder Mrs S. Butler.

permission to run a much-coveted Championship Show. Championship Shows attract a large entry and invariably the standard of entries can be much higher than at the other shows, probably including a number of cats that are Champions already, and even Grand Champions. Nevertheless, novices should never despise wins at Exemption and Sanction Shows. Such shows are excellent training both for the exhibitor and the exhibit.

Not all the clubs run shows, but a list of shows can be obtained from the GCCF secretary. It is also possible to get a list of clubs, with the names and addresses of the secretaries. If you intend to go in for breeding and showing, it is a good idea to join a club and to get to know members with similar interests. Some clubs run social events to help raise funds, and also arrange talks and teach-ins. Annual General Meetings are held once a year where members are elected to the committee and other offices. Members belonging to a club running a show may enter at reduced rates and compete for wins of cups and other specific prizes. Joining a club is the first step to becoming involved in the Cat Fancy, by helping at shows, giving out prize cards, helping on the awards tables and so on, possibly eventually stewarding, and ultimately becoming a judge, although this may take some years.

A breed club will look after the interests of a particular variety; one of the oldest clubs, for example, the Blue Persian Cat Society, was founded in 1901. The Society holds an annual Championship show and generally cares for anything appertaining to this variety. As planned breeding programmes bring new varieties into being, invariably new clubs are formed to promote them and to draw up standards that hopefully will eventually be passed by the genetics committee, and ultimately, the council. Once a provisional standard is granted a new variety may be shown in the Assessment Classes. In Assessment Classes each cat is judged individually by three judges. The cats are not competing against each other, and are judged by the provisional standard displayed on the pen. Merits are granted by judges if they consider the cats exhibited are up to the proposed standard. The club will encourage members to become involved in breeding programmes for such cats to increase the numbers shown and the Merits granted, so that full recognition will be given by the council in due course.

Self Chocolates are another recent variety — here is Etoile Chocolate Fancy, with a good coat. Owner and breeder Miss S.L. Booth.

Index

The numerals in **bold** type refer to the pages on which illustrations appear.

For further information on clubs and
societies worldwide please write to:
Mrs W. Davies, The Secretary, GCCF,
'Dovefields', Petworth Road, Witley,
Surrey GU8 5QW.